Kids Are
Tremendous!

By

Charlie "Tremendous" Jones

And

Bob Kelly

Kids Are Tremendous!

Published by
Executive Books
206 West Allen Street
Mechanicsburg, PA 17055
717-766-9499   800-233-2665
Fax: 717-766-6565
www.ExecutiveBooks.com

ISBN-10: 1-933715-64-2

ISBN-13: 978-1-933715-64-3

Printed in the United States of America

Kids Are *Tremendous!*

Table of Contents

1
Babies: Bits of Stardust

*Babies are bits of stardust
blown from the hand of God.
Lucky the woman who
knows the pangs of birth, for
she has held a star.*
–Larry Barratto

2
What Is a Child?

A child is the root of the heart.
–Carolina Maria de Jesus

3
From the Mouths of Babes

*Out of the mouths of babes
comes a lot of what they
should have swallowed.*
–Franklin P. Jones

4
Childhood: World of Wonder
Childhood is the world of miracle and wonder: as if creation rose, bathed in light, out of the darkness, utterly new and fresh and astonishing.
–Eugene Ionesco

5
Love and Praise: The Perfect Diet
Love your children with all your hearts…Praise them a lot. They live on it like bread and butter and they need it more than bread and butter.
–Lavina Christensen Fugal

6
Teaching Them What Counts
Teaching kids to count is fine, but teaching them what counts is best.
–Bob Talbert

7
Our Only Future
Kids are always the only future the human race has.
–William Saroyan

8
Discipline: By the Book

Mothers who raise
A child by the book
Can, if sufficiently vexed,
Hasten results
By applying the book
As well as the text.

–Evangelical Beacon

9
Our Best Teachers

When Gloria and I got married
and started our family, I
thought God gave me children
so I could teach them, but I
soon learned that God gave me
children so they could teach me!

–Charlie "Tremendous" Jones

10
You Can Say That Again!

The toughest thing about
raising kids is convincing
them you have seniority.

–Source Unknown

11
All Those Children

Gloria and I raised six kids,
all boys—except four! The
reason we had only six is be-
cause Gloria doesn't like kids.

–Charlie "Tremendous" Jones

_12_
Parents: Providing Roots and Wings

There are only two lasting
bequests we can hope to give
our children. One of these is
roots: the other wings.
—Hodding Carter

_13_
Girls: Little Bits of Heaven

A man who has only sons
and who has never fathered
a daughter has lost a little
bit of Heaven on earth.
—Irish Proverb

_14_
Boys: No Experience Needed

One of the best things in the
world is to be a boy; it
requires no experience, but
needs some practice to be a
good one.
—Charles Dudley Warner

_15_
Grandkids: God's Compensation

Grandchildren are God's
way of compensating us for
growing old.
—Mary H. Waldrip

_16_
Youth: Vanguard of Tomorrow
*Teenagers are the vanguard
of tomorrow. They are a
fresh breeze in a stale world.*
–Dan Valentine

_17_
Some "Handy" Advice
*Never raise your hand to
your children—it leaves
your midsection unprotected.*
–Robert Orben

_18_
Kids on Wry
*Ah, the patter of little feet
around the house. There's
nothing like having a midget
for a butler.*
–W.C. Fields

_19_
God's Apostles
*Children: God's apostles,
day by day sent forth to
preach of love, and hope,
and peace.*
–James Russell Lowell

20
Letter to a Grandson

When my first grandson was still a young boy, I wrote this letter to share with him some of the wonderful life lessons I've been learning.
–Charlie "Tremendous" Jones

21
Getting Kids to Read

You are the same today as you'll be in five years except for two things: the people you meet and the books you read.
–Charlie "Tremendous" Jones

Appendix

Acknowledgments

The selections in this book have been drawn from several hundred volumes in our personal libraries, and from other materials we have collected over many years, the sources of which were not always duly recorded. We have made every effort to give proper credit to the original authors of each selection, when known. In the event we have failed to acknowledge the correct source of any of this material, we sincerely apologize, and when such errors, if any, are called to our attention, we will make the appropriate corrections in future editions.

C.J. and B.K.

Kids Are *Tremendous!*

Foreword

By Charlie "Tremendous" Jones

One of the most *Tremendous* words in our vocabulary is "children." Just the mention or the thought of children brings to mind so many beautiful memories. As I reflected on the observations so many others have made about children, as recorded in this book, I thought back to my own childhood.

As soon as I was able to walk and talk, I began learning to act grown-up. I'd put my feet in my father's shoes, hold his pants up to my shoulders, and wonder, "Will I ever grow up?" As the years passed, I learned to act grown-up.

Then, when I was a young man, the grace of God revealed His love for me through His Son, Jesus Christ, and I began to live life all over again. This time, however, I didn't need to grow up but rather to decrease and celebrate every day as one of God's children.

It's been said that "the mark of smallness is a childish act; the mark of greatness is a childlike spirit." That's what this book is all about. Here in its pages there's something for everyone—to read, reread, memorize, realize and, especially, to share.

Kids Are *Tremendous!*

Introduction

By Bob Kelly

Every human being since Adam and Eve, billions of us, began life in the same way—as children. Many of us have gone on to have children, grandchildren, and perhaps even great grandchildren, of our own. Often to our chagrin, we've discovered that the experiences of childhood did little if anything to equip us to raise children. As parents, we've known headaches and heartaches, as we've ministered to the wounded knees and wounded hearts of our precious charges.

These are small prices to pay, however, for the joy of loving and being loved by children. At times confusing, frustrating, irritating, demanding and questioning, they are also invigorating, challenging, imaginative and heart-warming. And, generally, they're more than willing to forgive and forget the mistakes, even the awful ones, parents tend to make.

This is not a book of cute sayings by children but a collection of observations and advice about them made by hundreds of men and women over the past 3,000 years or so. In the following chapters, it covers such topics as infancy, training, communication, education, love, discipline, imagination and spirituality. There are the thought-provoking and the rib-tickling, the wise and the winsome, the delightful and the divine—more than 600 in all—enough to warm the heart of every reader.

Kids *are* tremendous and we trust every parent, grandparent, pastor, teacher, uncle, aunt and anyone else who has ever been a child, raised a child or tried to reason with a child, will enjoy these reminders of childhood, described by Eugene Ionesco as: "The world of miracle and wonder: as if creation rose, bathed in light, out of the darkness, utterly new and fresh and astonishing."

Chapter 1

Babies: Bits of Stardust

Babies are bits of stardust
blown from the hand of God.
Lucky the woman who
knows the pangs of birth, for
she has held a star.
–*Larry Barratto*

[Jesus said:] "A woman giving birth to a child has pain because her time has come; but when her baby is born she forgets the anguish because of her joy that a child is born into the world."
The Bible – John 16:21

Baby: an alimentary canal with a loud voice at one end and no sense of responsibility at the other.
Elizabeth I. Adamson

In every child who is born, under no matter what circumstances, and of no matter what parents, the potentiality of the human race is born again.
James Agee

When the first baby laughed for the first time, the laugh broke into a thousand pieces and they all went skipping about, and that was the beginning of fairies.
James M. Barrie

The first handshake in life is the greatest of all: the clasp of an infant fist around a parent's finger.
Mark Beltaire

Kids Are *Tremendous!*

Except that right side up is best, there is not much to learn about holding a baby. There are 152 distinctly different ways—and all are right! At least all will do.
Heywood Broun

I have never understood the fear of some parents about babies getting mixed up in the hospital. What difference does it make as long as you get a good one?
Heywood Broun

A baby is born with a need to be loved—and never outgrows it.
Frank A. Clark

As soon as I stepped out of my mother's womb onto dry land, I realized I had made a mistake—that I shouldn't have come, but the trouble with children is that they are not returnable.
Quentin Crisp

Babies are unreasonable; they expect far too much of existence. Each new generation that comes takes one look at the world, thinks wildly, "Is this all they've done to it?" and bursts into tears.
Clarence Day

Every baby born into the world is a finer one than the last.
Charles Dickens

Birth is the sudden opening of a window through which you look out upon a stupendous prospect. For what has happened? A miracle! You have exchanged nothing for the possibility of everything.
William M. Dixon

Kids Are *Tremendous!*

A child at birth has the capacity to become original. Or you can put him in a mold so that he will come out like everybody else.
Sylvanus and Evelyn Duvall

Here we have a baby. It is composed of a bald head and a pair of lungs.
Eugene Field

A man finds out what is meant by a spitting image when he tries to feed cereal to his infant.
Imogene Fry

Babies are such a nice way to start people.
Don Herold

The first home was made when a woman, cradling in her loving arms a baby, crooned a lullaby.
Elbert Hubbard

A child is helpless in inverse ratio to his age. He is at the zenith of his powers while he is an infant in arms. What on earth is more powerful than a very young baby?
Aline Kilmer

Baby: a tight little bundle of wailing and flannel.
Frederick Locker-Lampson

Giving birth is like trying to push a piano through a transom.
Alice Roosevelt Longworth

No baby is admired sufficiently to please the mother.
E.V. Lucas

Kids Are *Tremendous!*

…she who gives a baby birth,
Brings Saviour Christ again to earth.
John Masefield

A sweet, new blossom of Humanity,
Fresh fallen from God's own home to flower on earth.
Gerald Massey

Of all the joys that brighten suffering earth,
What joy is welcomed like a new-born child!
Caroline Norton

Getting down on all fours and imitating a rhinoceros stops babies from crying... Usually it makes the kid laugh. Sometimes it sends him into shock. Either way it quiets him down...Keep it up until the kid is a teenager and he definitely won't have his friends hanging around your house all the time.
P.J. O'Rourke

Babies are always more trouble than you thought—and more wonderful.
Charles Osgood

I think, at a child's birth, if a mother could ask a fairy godmother to endow it with the most useful gift, that gift would be curiosity.
Eleanor Roosevelt

A baby is God's opinion that life should go on...Never will a time come when the most marvelous recent invention is as marvelous as a newborn baby. The finest of our precision watches, the most super-colossal of our supercargo planes, don't compare with a newborn baby in the number and ingenuity of coils and springs, in the flow and change of

16

chemical solutions, in timing devices and interrelated parts that are irreplaceable.
Carl Sandburg

Happy child! The cradle is still to thee a vast space; but when thou art a man the boundless world will be too small for thee.
Johann Von Schiller

It sometimes happens, even in the best of families, that a baby is born. This is not necessarily a cause for alarm. The important thing is to keep your wits about you and borrow some money.
Elinor Goulding Smith

Making a decision to have a child—it's wondrous. It is to decide forever to have your heart go walking around outside your body.
Elizabeth Stone

Every child born is evidence that God is not yet discouraged of man.
Rabindranath Tagore

A babe in the house is a wellspring of pleasure, a messenger of peace and love, a resting place for innocence on earth, a link between angels and men.
Martin F. Tupper

A baby is an inestimable blessing and bother.
Mark Twain

The three most beautiful sights: a potato garden in bloom, a ship in sail, and a woman after the birth of her child.
Irish Proverb

Kids Are *Tremendous!*

A physician says babies don't need that traditional slap on the rear end when they're born. But at least it gives them an immediate idea of what life is going to be like.
Source Unknown

Most non-negotiable demand you'll ever hear: the baby calling for his 3 a.m. feeding.
Source Unknown

Chapter 2

What Is a Child?

A child is the root of the heart.
–*Carolina Maria de Jesus*

A child is a beam of sunlight from the Infinite and Eternal, with possibilities of virtue and vice—but as yet unstained.
Lyman Abbott

The child must know that he is a miracle; that since the beginning of the world there hasn't been, and until the end of the world there will not be, another child like him.
Pablo Casals

A child is a seed. You water it. You care for it the best you can. And then it grows all by itself into a beautiful flower.
Suzanne Chazin

A child is a curly, dimpled lunatic.
Ralph Waldo Emerson

A kid…is the last container of a sense of humor, which disappears as he gets older, and he laughs only according to the way the boss, society, politics, or race want him to. Then he becomes an adult. And an adult is an obsolete child.
Theodore Geisel [Dr. Seuss]

A child is a person who can't understand why someone would give away a perfectly good kitten.
Doug Larson

A child is a person who is going to carry on what you have

started...the fate of humanity is in his hands.
Abraham Lincoln

A child is not a vase to be filled, but a fire to be lit.
François Rabelais

Know what it is to be a child?...It is to believe in love, to
believe in loveliness, to believe in belief; it is to be so little
that the elves can reach to whisper in your ear; it is to turn
pumpkins into coaches, and mice into horses, lowness into
loftiness, and nothing into everything, for each child has its
fairy godmother in its own soul.
Francis Thompson

Children are the living messages we send to a time we will
not see.
John W. Whitehead

A child is like an axe; even if it hurts you, you still carry it
on your shoulder.
African Proverb

A child is someone who passes through your life and then
disappears into an adult.
Source Unknown

A child is an island of curiosity surrounded by a sea of
question marks.
Source Unknown

Chapter 3

From the Mouths of Babes

Out of the mouths of babes
comes a lot of what they
should have swallowed.
–*Franklin P. Jones*

Pretty much all the honest truthtelling there is in the world
is done by children.
Oliver Wendell Holmes

Children seldom misquote you. They more often repeat
word for word what you shouldn't have said.
Mae Maloo

To get his goodnight kiss he stood
Beside my chair one night
And raised an eager face to me,
A face with love alight.
And as I gathered in my arms
The son God gave to me,
I thanked my lad for being good,
And hoped he'd always be.
His little arms crept round my neck,
And then I heard him say
Four simple words I can't forget –
Four words that made me pray.
They turned a mirror on my soul,
On secrets no one knew,
They startled me, I hear them yet:
He said, "I'll be like you."
Herbert Parker

Kids Are *Tremendous!*

I remember seeing a picture of an old man addressing a small boy. "How old are you?" "Well, if you go by what Mama says, I'm five. But if you go by the fun I've had, I'm most a hundred."
William Lyons Phelps

There are only two things a child will share willingly—communicable diseases and his mother's age.
Dr. Benjamin Spock

Children are very adept at comprehending modern statistics. When they say: "Everyone else is allowed to," it is usually based on a survey of one.
Paul Sweeney

Of listening children have your fears, for little pitchers have big ears.
Dutch Proverb

What the child hears at the fireside is soon known at the parish church.
French Proverb

Martha had been naughty at school and was sent home with a note to her mother. By way of punishment, she was compelled to eat her dinner alone at a little table in the corner of the dining room. The rest of the family ignored her; until, that is, they heard her audibly delivering grace over her own meal. "I thank Thee, Lord Jesus," she intoned, "for preparing a table before me in the presence of mine enemies!"
Source Unknown

A woman invited some people to dinner. At the table, she asked her six-year-old daughter to ask the blessing. "I don't

know what to say," the child said." Just repeat what you here Mommy say," was the reply. The little girl bowed her head and prayed: "Dear Lord, why in the world did I invite all these people to dinner?"
Source Unknown

A little boy came up to the pastor and said: "Preacher, When I grow up, I'm going to give you half of all the money I make." The pastor said: "That's wonderful, but why do you want to do that?" The boy replied: "Because my dad says you're the poorest preacher he's ever known."
Source Unknown

Tots who started kindergarten at a certain elementary school came home the first day with a special note from the teacher, which read in part: "If you promise not to believe everything your child says happens at school, I'll promise not to believe everything he says happens at home."
Source Unknown

Chapter 4

Childhood: World of Wonder

*Childhood is the world of
miracle and wonder: as if
creation rose, bathed in
light, out of the darkness,
utterly new and fresh and
astonishing.*
–Eugene Ionesco

There is in most men's minds a secret instinct of reverence and affection towards the days of their childhood. They cannot help sighing with regret and tenderness when they think of it.
Saint Ailred of Rievaulx

Backward, turn backward, O Time, in your flight,
Make me a child again just for tonight!
Elizabeth Chase Akers

When childhood dies, its corpses are called adults and they enter society, one of the politer names of hell. That is why we dread children, even if we love them. They show us the state of our decay.
Brian Aldiss

Blessed be childhood, which brings down something of heaven into the midst of our rough earthliness.
Henri-Frédéric Amiel

Childhood and genius have the same master-organ in common—inquisitiveness. Let childhood have its way, and as it began where genius begins, it may find what genius finds.
Edward Bulwer-Lytton

Kids Are *Tremendous!*

The life of a little child is expectant, full of wonder, and free from self-consciousness.
Oswald Chambers

A little child is certain about his parents, but uncertain about everything else, therefore it lives a perfectly delightful healthy life.
Oswald Chambers

A child's life has no dates, it is free, silent, dateless. A child's life ought to be a child's life, full of simplicity.
Oswald Chambers

The child-heart is open to any and all avenues; an angel would no more surprise it than a man. In dreams, in visions, in visible and invisible ways, God can talk and reveal Himself to a child; but this profound yet simple way is lost for ever immediately we lose the open, childlike nature.
Oswald Chambers

The illusions of childhood are necessary experiences: a child should not be denied a balloon because an adult knows that sooner or later it will burst.
Marcelene Cox

The dreams of childhood—its airy fables; its graceful, beautiful, humane, impossible adornments of the world beyond: so good to be believed in once, so good to be remembered when outgrown.
Charles Dickens

I believe the power of observation in numbers of very small children to be quite wonderful for its closeness and accuracy.
Charles Dickens

Kids Are *Tremendous!*

Childhood, the bud of life, unfolding forms the youth; full-blown, becomes a man.
Ella E. Dodson

For me, the greatest tragedy of life is that childhood is such a short part of our lives.
Henry Dormann

In the man whose childhood has known caresses and kindness, there is always a fibre of memory that can be touched to gentle issues.
George Eliot

There is always one moment in childhood when the door opens and lets the future in.
Graham Greene

Time always seems long to the child who is waiting—for Christmas, for next summer, for becoming a grownup; long also when he surrenders his whole soul to each moment of a happy day.
Dag Hammerskjöld

Oh, when I was a tiny boy
My days and nights were full of joy.
My mates were blithe and kind!
No wonder that I sometimes sigh
And dash the tear drop from my eye
To cast a look behind!
Thomas Hood

I wonder if we who have grown up will ever know on this side of the grave how much we owe to children, who seem, but only seem, to owe us so much.
Francis C. Kelley

Kids Are *Tremendous!*

The primary need of children is not better laws or public programs. It is better childhoods.
Jack Kemp

Children think not of what is past, nor what is to come, but enjoy the present time, which few of us do.
Jean de La Bruyere

Curiosity in children is but an appetite for knowledge. One great reason why children abandon themselves wholly to silly pursuits and trifle their time away insipidly is because they find their curiosity balked, and their inquiries neglected.
John Locke

Of all people, children are the most imaginative.
Thomas Macaulay

Childhood: the kingdom where nobody dies.
Edna St. Vincent Millay

The childhood shows the man,
As morning shows the day.
John Milton

We call a child's mind "small" simply by habit; perhaps it is larger than ours, for it can take in almost anything without effort.
Christopher Morley

Hors d'oeuvres have always had a pathetic interest for me: they remind me of one's childhood that one goes through, wondering what the next course is going to be like—and during the rest of the menu wishes one had eaten more of the hors d'oeuvres.
H.H. Munro (Saki)

Kids Are *Tremendous!*

A child's eyes! Those clear wells of undefiled thought!
What on earth can be more beautiful? Full of hope, love,
and curiosity, they meet your own. In prayer, how earnest!
In joy, how sparkling! In sympathy, how tender!
Caroline Norton

Anybody who has survived his childhood has enough information about life to last him the rest of his days.
Flannery O'Connor

The plays of natural lively children are the infancy of art.
Children live in a world of imagination and feeling. They
invest the most insignificant object with any form they
please, and see in it whatever they wish to see.
Adam Oehlenschlager

Every child is an artist. The problem is how to remain an
artist once he grows up.
Pablo Picasso

The truth is children are not half-men and half-women, or
half-boys and half-girls. They are a race of beings themselves. And it is in the power of this curious race of beings
to plunge into the secret of life more deeply than all other
mortals.
J.C. Powys

Indeed, now that I come to think of it, I never really feel
grown-up at all. Perhaps this is because childhood, catching our imagination when it is fresh and tender, never lets
go of us.
J.B. Priestly

Children are entitled to their otherness, as anyone is; and
when we reach them, as we sometimes do, it is generally on

a point of sheer delight, to us so astonishing, but to them so
natural.
Alastair Reed

The whole difference between a man of genius and other
men…is that the former remains in great part a child, seeing with the large eyes of children, in perpetual wonder.
John Ruskin

Childhood is like a mirror which reflects in afterlife the im-
ages presented to it.
Samuel Smiles

Child desires are eternal and seldom yield to the lapse of
time.
Dr. Wilhelm Stekhel

It is true that a child is always hungry all over; but he is
also curious all over, and his curiosity is excited about as
early as his hunger.
Charles Dudley Warner

Childhood is frequently a solemn business for those inside it.
George F. Will

Sweet childish days, that were so long
As twenty days are now.
William Wordsworth

The wondrous adventures a child's mind can experience on
a walk through a deserted, littered lot between two old
houses.
Source Unknown

Chapter 5

Love and Praise: The Perfect Diet

*Love your children with all
your hearts...Praise them a
lot. They live on it like bread
and butter and they need it
more than bread and butter.*
–Lavina Christensen Fugal

"And whoever welcomes a little child like this in my name welcomes me [Jesus]."
The Bible – Matthew 18:5

Happy are the families where the government of parents is the reign of affection, and obedience of the children the submission of love.
Francis Bacon

No one who has ever brought up a child can doubt for a moment that love is literally the life-giving fluid of human existence.
Dr. Smiley Blanton

Loving a child doesn't mean giving in to all his whims; to love him is to bring out the best in him, to teach him to love what is difficult.
Nadia Boulanger

Words of praise, indeed, are almost as necessary to warm a child into congenial life as acts of kindness and affection. Judicious praise is to children what sun is to flowers.
Christian N. Bovée

Kids Are *Tremendous!*

The purest affection the heart can hold is the honest love of a nine-year-old.
Holman F. Day

I love these little people; and it is not a slight thing when they, who are so fresh from God, love us.
Charles Dickens

Love children especially, for...they live to soften and purify our hearts, and, as it were, to guide us.
Feodor Dostoevsky

In praising or loving a child, we love and praise not that which is, but that which we hope for.
Johann von Goethe

Only as genuine Christian holiness, and Christlike love are expressed in the life of a parent, can the child have the opportunity to inherit the flame and not the ashes.
Stephen G. Green

Love equally all your children. Sometimes the favored disappoint, and the neglected make you happy.
Berekia HaNakdan

The best smell is bread, the best savour salt, the best love that of children.
George Herbert

Children need love, especially when they do not deserve it.
Harold S. Hulbert

If a child lives with approval, he learns to like himself.
Dorothy Nolte

31

Kids Are *Tremendous!*

Once you've loved a child, you love all children. You give your love away to one, and you find that by the giving you have made yourself an inexhaustible treasury.
    Margaret Lee Runbeck

Give a little love to a child, and you get a great deal back.
    John Ruskin

Nature kindly warps our judgment about our children, especially when they are young, when it would be a fatal thing for them if we did not love them.
    George Santayana

Call not that man wretched who, whatever ills he suffers, has a child to love.
    Robert Southey

A child may not be as good as you tell him he is, but he'll try harder thereafter.
    Source Unknown

Chapter 6

Teaching Them What Counts

Teaching kids to count is
fine, but teaching them what
counts is best.
–Bob Talbert

Only be careful and watch yourselves closely so that you do not forget the things your eyes have seen or let them slip from your heart as long as you live. Teach them to your children and to their children after them.
The Bible – Deuteronomy 4:9

These commandments that I give you today are to be upon your hearts. Impress them on your children. Talk about them when you sit at home and when you walk along the road, when you lie down and when you get up.
The Bible – Deuteronomy 6:6,7

Train a child in the way he should go, and when he is old he will not turn from it.
The Bible – Proverbs 22:6

Fathers, do not exasperate your children; instead, bring them up in the training and instruction of the Lord.
The Bible – Ephesians 6:4

The Hebrew word for parents is *horim*, and it comes from the same root as *moreh*, teacher. The parent is, and remains, the first and most important teacher that the child will ever have.
Rabbi Kassel Abelson

Kids Are *Tremendous!*

Children have never been very good at listening to their elders, but they have never failed to imitate them.
James Baldwin

Training a baby by the book is a good idea, only you need a different book for each baby.
Dan Bennett

Ideals and principles continue from generation to generation only when they are built into the hearts of children as they grow up.
George S. Benson

If we paid no more attention to our plants than we do to our children, we would now be living in a jungle of weeds.
Luther Burbank

Let every father and mother realize that when their child is three years of age, they have done more than half they will ever do for his character.
Horace Bushnell

The most important thing that parents can teach their children is how to get along without them.
Frank A. Clark

In their eagerness for their children to acquire skills and to succeed, parents may forget that youngsters need time to think, and privacy in which to do it.
James Cox

Children just don't fit into a "to do" list very well. It takes time to be an effective parent when children are small. It takes time to introduce them to good books—it takes time to fly kites and play punch ball and put together jigsaw

puzzles. It takes time to listen.
Dr. James Dobson

Kids can frustrate and irritate their parents...but the rewards of raising them far outweigh the cost. Besides, nothing worth having ever comes cheap.
Dr. James Dobson

Religious words have value to the child only as experience in the home gives them meaning.
John Drescher

If I were asked what single qualification was necessary for one who has the care of children, I should say patience—patience with their tempers, with their understandings, with their progress...patience to go over first principles again and again; steadily to add a little every day; never to be irritated by wilful or accidental hindrance.
François de la Fenelon

The essence of our effort to see that every child has a chance must be to assure each an equal opportunity, not to become equal, but to become different—to realize whatever unique potential of body, mind and spirit he or she possesses.
John Fischer

Upon our children—how they are taught—rests the fate—or fortune—of tomorrow's world.
B.C. Forbes

Teach your child to hold his tongue; he'll learn fast enough to speak.
Benjamin Franklin

Almost every child would learn to write sooner if allowed to do his homework in wet cement.
Haim Ginott

The family fireside is the best of schools.
Arnold H. Glasow

How many hopes and fears, how many ardent wishes and anxious apprehensions are twisted together in the threads that connect the parent to the child.
Samuel Griswold Goodrich

I think that saving a little child
And bringing him to his own,
Is a derned sight better business
Than loafing around the throne.
John Hay

Virtue and a trade are the best inheritance for children.
George Herbert

An infallible way to make your child miserable is to satisfy all his demands.
Henry Home

If telling were teaching my child would be perfect.
William L. Howse

Babies do not want to hear about babies; they like to be told of giants and castles, and of somewhat which can stretch and stimulate their little minds.
Samuel Johnson

Children have more need of models than of critics.
Joseph Joubert

Kids Are *Tremendous!*

Our greatest obligation to our children is to prepare them to understand and to deal effectively with the world in which they will live and not with the world we have known or the world we would prefer to have.

Grayson Kirk

Children are not things to be molded, but are people to be unfolded.

Jess Lair

As very rough weather destroys the buds of spring, so does too early an experience of life's hard toil blight the young promise of a child's faculties, and renders any true education impossible.

Pope Leo III

Too often we give children answers to remember rather than problems to solve.

Roger Lewin

None of the things children are to learn should ever be made a burden to them, or imposed on them as a task.

John Locke

Children generally hate to be idle. All the care then should be that their busy humor should be constantly employed in something that is of use to them.

John Locke

A torn jacket is soon mended, but hard words bruise the heart of a child.

Henry Wadsworth Longfellow

The important thing is not so much that every child should

be taught, as that every child should be given the wish to
learn.
John Lubbock

Would you write your name among the stars?
Then write it large upon
The hearts of children.
They will remember!
Have you visions of a nobler, happier world?
Tell the children!
They will build it for you.
Clara Tree Major

Children, not knowing that they are having an easy time,
have a good many hard times. Growing and learning and
obeying the rules of their elders, or fighting against them,
are not easy things to do.
Don Marquis

We want our children to grow up to be such persons that ill-
fortune, if they meet with it, will bring out strength in them,
and that good fortune will not trip them up, but make them
winners.
Edward Sandford Martin

Lord, give to men who are old and rougher
the things that little children suffer,
And let keep bright and undefiled
the young years of the little child.
John Masefield

The hearts of small children are delicate organs. A cruel beginning in this world can twist them into curious shapes.
Carson McCullers

Kids Are *Tremendous!*

Likely as not, the child you can do the least with will do the most to make you proud.
Mignon McLaughlin

Every child is born with a great capacity for knowledge…We must create interest in the heart and mind of the child that will make him reach out and take hold upon the things he is taught.
Henrietta Mears

By the time children are five, their parents will have done at least half of all that can ever be done to determine their children's future faith.
Randolph Miller

We can't give our children the future, strive though we may to make it secure. But we can give them the present.
Kathleen Norris

The conscience of children is formed by the influences that surround them; their notions of good and evil are the result of the moral atmosphere they breathe.
Johann Richter

To be able to endure is the first lesson which a child ought to learn, and the one which it will have the most need to know.
Jean-Jacques Rousseau

There is no absurdity so palpable but that it can be planted in the human head if only you begin to inculcate it before the age of five, by constantly repeating it with an air of great solemnity.
Arthur Schopenhauer

Every child has a right to be both well fed and well led.
Ruth Smelter

We are apt to forget that children watch examples better than they listen to preaching.
Roy L. Smith

With children we must mix gentleness with firmness; they must not always have their own way, but they must not always be thwarted. If we have never had headaches through rebuking them, we shall have headaches when they grow up.
Charles H. Spurgeon

Children develop character by what they see, by what they hear, and by what they are repeatedly led to do.
James Stenson

It's a great mistake, I think, to put children off with false-hoods and nonsense, when their growing powers of observation and discrimination excite in them a desire to know about things.
Annie Sullivan

It needs courage to let our children go, but we are trustees and stewards and have to hand them back to life—to God. As the old saying puts it: "What I gave I have." We have to love them and lose them.
Alfred Torrie

Parents must not cowardly abdicate their authority...In the struggle, the child will acquire experience; he will learn how far he may resist and at what point he must submit.
Paul Tournier

Kids Are *Tremendous!*

Every word and deed of a parent is a fibre woven into the character of a child, which ultimately determines how that child fits into the fabric of society.
  David Wilkerson

The hardest part of raising children is teaching them to ride bicycles…A shaky child on a bicycle for the first time needs both support and freedom. The realization that this is what the child will always need can hit hard.
  Sloan Wilson

The important thing is that children should grow up with parents who believe that there are some ways of life which for us today are better than others and that these ways are worth defending with every ounce of our strength.
  Anna W.M. Wolf

A child's life is like a piece of paper on which each passerby leaves a mark.
  Chinese Proverb

Fifty years from now, it will not matter what kind of car you drove, what kind of house you lived in, how much you had in your bank account, nor what your clothes looked like. But the world will be a little better place because you were important in the life of a child.
  Source Unknown

Children are inclined to learn from television [because] it is never too busy to talk to them, and it never has to brush them aside while it does household chores.
  Source Unknown

Everybody seems to know how to raise other people's children
  Source Unknown

When a child asks difficult questions, invention is the necessity of mother.
Source Unknown

The kind of person your child is going to be, he is already becoming.
Source Unknown

Chapter 7

Our Only Future

Kids are always the only
future the human race has.
–William Saroyan

At that time Jesus said, "I praise you, Father, Lord of
heaven and earth, because you have hidden these things
from the wise and learned, and revealed them to little
children."
    The Bible – Matthew 11:25

He [Jesus] called a little child and had him stand among
them. And he said: "I tell you the truth, unless you change
and become like little children, you will never enter the
kingdom of heaven."
    The Bible – Matthew 18:2-3

Jesus said: "Let the little children come to me, and do not
hinder them, for the kingdom of heaven belongs to such as
these."
    The Bible – Matthew 19:14

I have often thought what a melancholy world this would
be without children.
    Samuel Taylor Coleridge

A world without children is a world without newness,
regeneration, color, and vigor.
    Dr. James Dobson

The soul is healed by being with children.
    Feodor Dostoevsky

Kids Are *Tremendous!*

The most turbulent, the most restless child, has, in the midst of all his faults, something true, ingenuous, and natural, which is of infinite value, and merits every respect.
  Felix A. Dupanloup

His soul is yet a white paper unscribbled with observations of the world, wherewith, at length, it becomes a blurred note-book.
  Bishop Earle

Who is not attracted by bright and pleasant children, to prattle, to creep, and to play with them?
  Epictetus

How delicate the skin, how sweet the breath of children!
  Euripides

For such a child I bless God, in whose bosom he is! May I and mine become as this little child.
  John Evelyn

For children is there any happiness which is not also noise?
  Frederick W. Faber

Children—the fruit of the seeds of all your finest hopes.
  Gloria Gaither

You are the bows from which your children as living arrows are sent forth.
  Kahlil Gibran

Children, like dogs, have so sharp a scent that they detect everything—the bad before all the rest.
  Johann von Goethe

Kids Are *Tremendous!*

When we are confused by the world, we can gain a renewed feeling of security from seeing the light in the eyes of a happy, trusting child.
Harry Hepner

What feeling is so nice as a child's hand in yours? So small, so soft and warm, like a kitten huddling in the shelter of your clasp.
Marjorie Holmes

One laugh of a child will make the holiest day more sacred still.
Robert G. Ingersoll

If children knew, oh, if they only knew their power! It is something absolutely glorious in its immensity. But they do not even see it dimly until it is gone forever.
Aline Kilmer

Where children are, there is the golden age.
Novalis

Oh, grown-ups cannot understand,
And grown-ups never will,
How short the way to fairyland
Across the purple hill.
Alfred Noyes

When I approach a child, he inspires in me two sentiments: tenderness for what he is, and respect for what he may become.
Louis Pasteur

Some of my best friends are children. In fact, all of my best friends are children.
J.D. Salinger

Kids Are *Tremendous!*

Children are the keys of paradise.
Richard Henry Stoddard

There are no seven wonders of the world in the eyes of a child. There are seven million.
Walt Streightiff

It's not easy to be crafty and winsome at the same time, and few accomplish it after the age of six.
D. Sutten

Children have but little charity for one another's defects.
Mark Twain

The whole idea that children should be seen and not heard is archaic. Young people are not extensions of our egos, they are individuals unto themselves.
Henry Winkler

Children are not things to be molded but are people to be unfolded.
Source Unknown

Children are messengers we send to a time we will not see.
Source Unknown

I Saw Tomorrow Look at Me
I saw tomorrow marching
On little children's feet;
Within their forms and faces read
Her prophecy complete.

I saw tomorrow look at me
From little children's eyes;
And thought how carefully we'd teach
If we were really wise.
Source Unknown

Chapter 8

Discipline: By the Book

Mothers who raise
A child by the book
Can, if sufficiently vexed,
Hasten results
By applying the book
As well as the text.
–Evangelical Beacon

Discipline your son, and he will give you peace; he will
bring delight to your soul.
The Bible – Proverbs 29:17

Whenever a child lies, you will always find a severe parent.
A lie would have no sense unless the truth were felt to be
dangerous.
Alfred Adler

It is ominous for the future of a child when the discipline he
receives is based on the emotional needs of the disciplinar-
ian rather than on any consideration of the child's own
needs.
Gordon W. Allport

I read one psychologist's theory that said, "Never strike a
child in anger." When should I strike him? When he is kiss-
ing me on my birthday? When he is recuperating from the
measles? Do I slap the Bible out of his hand on a Sunday?
Erma Bombeck

To discipline a child is not to punish him for stepping out of
line, but to teach that child the way he ought to go. Disci-

pline therefore includes everything that you do in order to help children learn.
Henry R. Brandt

Reprimand not a child immediately on the offence. Wait till the irritation has been replaced by serenity.
Moses Hasid

The antidote for crime should be administered in childhood, by the parents. The problem is not fundamentally that of the improper child so much as it is that of the improper home.
John W. Hill

Children want some honest direction. They want a set of sensible rules to live by. The time has come to dust off the rule book.
Jenkins Lloyd Jones

When a child can be brought to tears, not from fear of punishment, but from repentance for his offence, he needs no chastisement. When the tears begin to flow from grief at one's own conduct, be sure there is an angel nestling in the bosom.
A. Mann

Where does discipline end? Where does cruelty begin? Somewhere between these, thousands of children inhabit a voiceless hell.
François Mauriac

To refuse to discipline a child is to refuse a clear demand of God, for a child who doesn't obey both parents will find it much harder to learn to obey God.
Kenneth Taylor

Kids Are *Tremendous!*

If you can't beat sense into one's head,
Try the other end instead.
  Russian Proverb

Love your children with your heart, but teach them with
your hand.
  Russian Proverb

The actions of some children today suggest that their parents embarked upon the sea of matrimony without a paddle.
  Source Unknown

Chapter 9

Our Best Teachers

When Gloria and I got married and started our family, I thought God gave me children so I could teach them, but I soon learned that God gave me children so they could teach me!
–Charlie "Tremendous" Jones

An adult may see human wisdom manifested in its highest form by watching a child's boundless capacity for making the most of today.
O.A. Battista

There are many things I admire in children, but the one that impresses me the most is the way they can get the thrill of a lifetime out of the little things that we adults usually can't be bothered with.
O.A. Battista

The parents exist to teach the child, but also they must learn what the child has to teach them; and the child has a very great deal to teach them.
Arnold Bennett

The Road to Laughtertown
Would ye learn the road to Laughtertown,
O ye who have lost the way?
Would ye have young heart though your hair be gray?
Go learn from a little child each day,
Go serve his wants and play his play,

50

And catch the lilt of his laughter gay,
And follow his dancing feet as they stray;
For he knows the road to Laughtertown,
O ye who have lost the way.
Katherine D. Blake

For a person in rugged health who is not particularly
dressed up and does not want to write a letter or read the
newspaper, we can imagine few diversions more enjoyable
than to have a child turned loose on him.
Heywood Broun

If a child is to keep alive his inborn sense of wonder…he
needs the companionship of at least one adult who can
share it, rediscovering with him the joy, excitement and
mystery of the world we live in.
Rachel Carson

Every adult needs a child to teach; it's the way adults learn.
Frank A. Clark

One of the most visible effects of a child's presence in the
household is to turn the parents into complete idiots when, without him, they would perhaps have remained mere imbeciles.
Georges Courteline

Who of us is mature enough for offspring before the offspring themselves arrive? The value of marriage is not that
adults produce children but that children produce adults.
Peter De Vries

There are many things that we get from our children, in-
cluding love and meaning and purpose and an opportunity
to give. They help us to maintain our sense of humor.
Dr. James Dobson

Kids Are *Tremendous!*

We try to make our children become more like us, instead of trying to become more like them—with the result that we pick up none of their good traits, and they pick up most of our bad ones.
Sydney J. Harris

Some wonder that children should be given to young mothers. But what instruction does the babe bring to the mother! She learns patience, self-control, endurance; her very arm grows strong so that she can hold the dear burden longer than the father can.
T.W. Higginson

It is the malady of our age that the young are so busy teaching us that they have no time left to learn.
Eric Hoffer

The real menace in dealing with a five-year-old is that in no time at all you begin to sound like a five-year-old.
Jean Kerr

Everyone likes to think that he has done reasonably well in life, so it comes as a shock to find our children believing differently. The temptation is to tune them out; it takes much more courage to listen.
John D. Rockefeller III

Grown-ups never understand anything for themselves, and it is tiresome for children to be always and forever explaining things to them.
Antoine de Saint-Exupéry

Parents learn a lot from their children about coping with life.
Muriel Sparks

Having a young child explain something exciting he has
seen is the finest example of communication you will ever
see or hear.
Bob Talbert

To a child, its games of make-believe are as serious as our
realities are to us. I sometimes wonder which of the two has
more substance.
Source Unknown

Small girl's essay on parents: "The trouble with parents is
that they are so old when we get them, it's hard to change
their habits."
Source Unknown

If children never asked questions, they would never learn
how little we adults know.
Source Unknown

The most powerful combination of emotions in the world is
not called out by any cosmic event, nor is it found in novels
or history books; merely, it is found by a parent gazing
down upon a sleeping child.
Source Unknown

Chapter 10

You Can Say That Again!

*The toughest thing about
raising kids is convincing
them you have seniority.*
–Source Unknown

In case you're worried about what's going to become of the younger generation, it's going to grow up and start worrying about the younger generation.
Roger Allen

Start a program for gifted children, and every parent demands that his child should be enrolled.
Thomas Bailey

Our children are not going to be just "our children"—they are going to be other people's husbands and wives and the parents of our grandchildren.
Mary S. Calderone

If you treat a sick child like and adult and a sick adult like a child, everything usually works out pretty well.
Ruth Carlisle

There's nothing that can help you understand your beliefs more than trying to explain them to an inquisitive child.
Frank A. Clark

Better to be driven out from among men than to be disliked of children.
Richard Henry Dana

Kids Are *Tremendous!*

When children sound silly, you will always find that it is an imitation of their elders.
Ernest Dimnet

Children are very nice observers, and will often perceive your slightest defect.
François de la Fenelon

If children grew up according to early indications, we should have nothing but geniuses.
Johann von Goethe

Most of us don't expect to be admired by our children, but we wouldn't mind just a slight closing of the generation gap.
Troy Gordon

Children are born optimists, and we slowly educate them out of their heresy.
Louise Imogene Guiney

Children have more energy after a hard day of play than they do after a good night's sleep.
Dr. R.F. Gumperson

There is little use to talk about your child to anyone; other people either have one or haven't.
Don Herold

The business of being a child interests a child not at all. Children very rarely play at being other children.
David Hollaway

A child enters your home and makes so much noise for twenty years that you can hardly stand it; then departs leav-

ing your house so silent that you think you will go mad.
John Andrew Holmes

One of the most obvious facts about grown-ups to a child is
that they have forgotten what it is like to be a child.
Randall Jarrell

Children have an unerring instinct for when they are being
patronized. They go immediately on the defensive against
head-patting adults who treat them like strange beings.
Art Linkletter

The car trip can draw the family together, as it was in the
days before television when parents and children actually
talked to each other.
Andrew H. Malcolm

Children are very much like airplanes; you hear only of the
ones that crash.
E.C. McKenzie

The healthy human child will keep
Away from home, except to sleep.
Were it not for the common cold,
Our young we never would behold.
Ogden Nash

Television has changed the American child from an irre-
sistible force into an immovable object.
Laurence Peter

As we read the school reports upon our children, we realize
with a sense of relief that can rise to delight that—thank
Heaven—nobody is reporting in this fashion upon us.
J.B. Priestly

Kids Are *Tremendous!*

Richman's Inevitables of Parenthood: (1) Enough is never enough. (2) The sun always rises in the baby's bedroom window. (3) Birthday parties always end in tears. (4) Whenever you decide to take the kids home, it is always five minutes earlier that they break into fights, tears, hysteria.
> *Phyllis C. Richman*

The surest way to make it hard for children is to make it easy for them.
> *Eleanor Roosevelt*

You are worried about seeing him spend his early years in doing nothing. What! Is it nothing to be happy? Nothing to skip, play and run around all day long? Never in his life will he be so busy again.
> *Jean-Jacques Rousseau*

Parents no longer bring children up; they finance them.
> *Joseph Salak*

Children require guidance and sympathy far more than instruction.
> *Annie Sullivan*

A food is not necessarily essential just because your child hates it.
> *Katherine Whitehorn*

No symphony orchestra ever played music like a two-year-old girl laughing with a puppy.
> *Bern Williams*

The factory that produces the most important product is the home.
> *Carol Williams*

Kids Are *Tremendous!*

Give to a pig when it grunts and to a child when it cries, and you'll have a fine pig and a bad child.
Danish Proverb

Small children don't let you sleep; big children don't let you rest.
Yiddish Proverb

There's nothing thirstier than a child who has just gone to bed.
Source Unknown

We were kids when everything was the kids' fault. Now we're parents and everything is the parents' fault.
Source Unknown

If you think practice makes perfect, the chances are that you never had a child taking music lessons.
Source Unknown

A truly rich man is one whose children run into his arms when his hands are empty.
Source Unknown

Kids are confused. Half of the adults tell him to find himself; the other half tell him to get lost.
Source Unknown

The quickest way to get a child's attention is to take a nap.
Source Unknown

Children are little bonds who hold a marriage together by keeping their parents too busy to quarrel with each other.
Source Unknown

Kids Are *Tremendous!*

Nearly every man is a firm believer in heredity until his son makes a fool of himself.

Source Unknown

Chapter 11

All Those Children

Gloria and I raised six
kids, all boys—except four!
The reason we had only six
is because Gloria doesn't
like kids.
–Charlie "Tremendous" Jones

God blessed them and said to them, "Be fruitful and increase in number..."
The Bible – Genesis 1:28

Sons are a heritage from the Lord, children are a reward
from him...Blessed is the man whose quiver is full of them.
The Bible – Psalm 127:3, 5

You should have seen what a fine-looking man he was before he had all those children.
Arapesh tribesman

A father of five boys will hardly agree that there is safety in
numbers.
O.A. Battista

There are two things in this life for which we are never
fully prepared: twins.
Josh Billings

I have over 42,000 children, and not one comes to visit.
Mel Brooks (as the 2,000-Year-Old Man)

Children in a family are like flowers in a bouquet: there's

always one determined to face in the opposite direction
from the way the arranger desires.

Marcelene Cox

The beauty of "spacing" children many years apart lies in
the fact that parents have time to learn the mistakes that
were made with the older ones—which permits them to
make exactly the opposite mistakes with the younger ones.

Sydney J. Harris

Raising children is like making biscuits: it is as easy to
raise a big batch as one, while you have your hands in the
dough.

E.W. Howe

For unflagging interest and enjoyment, a household of children, if things go reasonably well, certainly makes all other
forms of success and achievement lose their importance by
comparison.

Theodore Roosevelt

[In a big family] the first child is kind of like the first pan-
cake. If it's not perfect, that's okay, there are a lot more
coming.

Justice Antonin Scalia

There is more happiness in a multitude of children than
safety in a multitude of counselors; and if I were a rich
man, I should like to have twenty children.

Sydney Smith

I was once present when an old mother, who had brought
up a large family of children with eminent success, was
asked by a young one what she would recommend in the
case of some children who were too anxiously educated,

and her reply was—"I think, my dear, a little wholesome neglect."
Sir Henry Taylor

As long as you are in your right mind don't you ever pray for twins. Twins amount to a permanent riot. And there ain't no real difference between triplets and an insurrection.
Mark Twain

Before I got married I had six theories about bringing up children; now I have six children and no theories.
John Wilmot

A person with six children is better satisfied than a person with $6 million. Reason: The man with $6 million wants more.
Source Unknown

A five-year-old girl was asked by the minister how many children there were in the family. She replied, "Seven." The minister observed that so many children must cost a lot. "Oh, no," the child replied, "We don't buy 'em, we raise 'em."
Source Unknown

Chapter 12

Parents: Providing Roots and Wings

*There are only two lasting
bequests we can hope to give
our children. One of these is
roots: the other wings.*
–Hodding Carter

Any mother could perform the jobs of several air-traffic controllers with ease.
Lisa Alther

There must be such a thing as a child with average ability, but you can't find a parent who will admit that it is his child.
Thomas Bailey

Instant availability without continuous presence is probably the best role a mother can play.
Lotte Bailyn

The God to whom little boys say their prayers has a face very much like their mother's.
James M. Barrie

The other evening my son and I spent more than an hour having all kinds of fun blowing bubbles with what amounted to a penny's worth of soap solution. And then it occurred to me that the cost of a child's toys mean little or nothing to him in comparison with having his dad as a playmate
O.A. Battista

Kids Are *Tremendous!*

It is astonishing how many children work their way up to an honest manhood in spite of parents and friends.
Henry Ward Beecher

The mother's heart is the child's schoolroom.
Henry Ward Beecher

What parents do for their children is...infinitely more important and valuable than all things else.
Gertrude Berg

It is pretty generally agreed that all a woman needs to do to know all about children is to have some. This wisdom is attributed to instinct...I have seen mothers give beer and spaghetti and Neapolitan ice cream to children in arms, and if they got that from instinct the only conclusion possible is that instinct is not what it used to be.
Heywood Broun

Anyone who thinks mother love is as soft and golden-eyed as a purring cat should see a cat defending her kittens.
Pam Brown

A father is a man who expects his son to be as good a man as he meant to be.
Frank A. Clark

It is easy to pick the children whose mothers are good housekeepers; they are usually found in other people's yards.
Marcelene Cox

Every mother who has lost an infant has gained a child of immortal youth.
George William Curtis

Kids Are *Tremendous!*

A suburban mother's role is to deliver children obstetrically once, and by car for ever after.
Peter De Vries

Children want their parents more than the junk we buy them.
Dr. James Dobson

A woman never stops to consider how very uninteresting her children would be if they were some other woman's.
Robert C. Edwards

There never was a child so lovely but his mother was glad to get him asleep.
Ralph Waldo Emerson

Parents' influence is inevitable and continuous; they cannot be passive if they would. You cannot really neglect your children, but you can destroy them.
Frederick W. Faber

Among those things which are so simple that even a child can operate them are parents.
Arnold H. Glasow

Only mothers can think of the future, because they give birth to it in their children.
Maxim Gorky

If I cannot give my children a perfect mother I can at least give them more of the one they've got—and make that one more loving. I will be available. I will take time to listen, time to play, time to be home when they arrive from school, time to counsel and encourage.
Ruth Bell Graham

Kids Are *Tremendous!*

Only as genuine Christian holiness, and Christlike love are expressed in the life of a parent, can the child have the opportunity to inherit the flame and not the ashes.
Stephen G. Green

Fathers should never underestimate the priceless return they receive—both in this life and in the life to come—on time they invest in their children.
Chris Halverson

Could we understand half what mothers say and do to us when infants, we should be filled with such conceit of our own importance as would make us unsupportable through life. Happy the child whose mother is tired of talking nonsense to him before he is old enough to know the sense of it.
August W. Hare

A mother should give her children a superabundance of enthusiasm, that after they have lost all they are sure to lose on mixing with the world, enough may still remain to prompt and support them through great actions.
Julius C. Hare

The commonest fallacy among women is that simply having children makes one a mother—which is as absurd as believing that having a piano makes one a musician.
Sydney Harris

To be a successful father there's one absolute rule: when you have a kid, don't look at it for the first two years.
Ernest Hemingway

One father is more than a hundred schoolmasters.
George Herbert

The most important thing a father can do for his children is to love their mother.
Rev. Theodore M. Hesburgh

The hand of the parent writes on the heart of the child the first faint characters which time deepens into strength so that nothing can efface them.
Richard Hill

True parenthood is self-destructive. The wise parent is one who effectively does himself out of his job as parent. The silver cord must be broken. It must not be broken too abruptly, but it must be broken. The child must cease to be a child...The wise parent delivers his child over to society.
Robert Holmes

If there were no schools to take the children away from home part of the time, the insane asylum would be filled with mothers.
E.W. Howe

You never get over being a child, as long as you have a mother to go to.
Sarah Orne Jewett

Now, as always, the most automated appliance in a household is the mother.
Beverly Jones

Parents who expect gratitude from their children (there are even some who insist on it) are like usurers who gladly risk their capital if only they receive interest.
Franz Kafka

Kids Are *Tremendous!*

My father didn't tell me how to live; he lived, and let me watch him do it.

> *Clarence Budington Kelland*

For Any Mother Of A Small Boy
Was it for this I rendered sterile
Bottles, blankets and apparel,
Scrubbed and boiled and disinfected,
Let no one touch unless inspected,
That now, quite innocent of soap,
My erstwhile pride, my one-time hope,
In spite of all the books assert
Should thrive on good old-fashioned dirt?

> *Elizabeth-Ellen Long*

A parent must respect the spiritual person of his child, and approach it with reverence.

> *George MacDonald*

My mother loved children—she would have given anything if I had been one.

> *Groucho Marx*

Because I happen to be a parent of almost fiercely maternal nature, I praise casualness. It seems to me the rarest of virtues. It is useful enough when children are small. It is important to the point of necessity when they are adolescents.

> *Phyllis McGinley*

When their children fail to charm others, few parents can remain neutral.

> *Mignon McLaughlin*

The quickest way for a parent to get a child's attention is to

sit down and look comfortable.
  Lane Olinghouse

Every mother is like Moses. She does not enter the promised land. She prepares a world she will not see.
  Pope Paul VI

The only thing children wear out faster than shoes is parents.
  John J. Plomp

A wise mother's prayer: May my son grow up to be great enough to achieve world fame—and big enough not to be conscious of his greatness.
  J.A. Rosenkranz

Parental affection, when carried to excess and unrestrained by reason and piety, is the ruin of children, and renders them unfit for all doctrine and virtue.
  Christian Scriver

The best brought-up children are those who have seen their parents as they are. Hypocrisy is not the parents' first duty.
  George Bernard Shaw

Children are the anchors that hold a mother to life.
  Sophocles

A child is not likely to find a father in God unless he finds something of God in his father.
  Austin L. Sorenson

In automobile terms, the child supplies the power but the parents have to do the steering.
  Dr. Benjamin Spock

Kids Are *Tremendous!*

I don't think there are enough devils in hell to take a young person from the arms of a godly mother.
Billy Sunday

Mother is the name for God in the lips and hearts of little children.
William Makepeace Thackeray

Parenthood remains the greatest single preserve of the amateur.
Alvin Toffler

The biggest family problems are caused by know-it-all kids and yes-it-all parents.
Frank Tyger

Parents are the bones on which children cut their teeth.
Peter Ustinov

Parents of bright children are always great believers in heredity.
Pat Williams and Ken Hussar

There's only one pretty child in the world, and every mother has it.
English Proverb

Parents often talk about the younger generation as if they didn't have anything to do with it.
Funny, Funny World

The parent's life is the child's copybook.
Jewels of Home

A parent should never make distinctions between his children.
The Talmud

Kids Are *Tremendous!*

Don't be discouraged if your children reject your advice. Years later they will offer it to their own offspring.
Source Unknown

Parenting is hereditary. If your parents didn't have any children, you're not likely to have any either.
Source Unknown

When all the kids have grown up, married, and moved away, many parents experience a strange new emotion; it's called ecstasy.
Source Unknown

When a child pays attention to his parents, they're probably whispering.
Source Unknown

Any father who thinks he's all-important should remind himself that this country honors fathers only one day a year while pickles get a whole week.
Source Unknown

By the time a man realizes that maybe his father was right, he usually has a son who thinks he's wrong.
Source Unknown

A sweater is a garment worn by a child when his mother feels chilly.
Source Unknown

A father is one whose daughter marries a man who is vastly her inferior mentally, but then gives birth to unbelievably brilliant grandchildren.
Source Unknown

Chapter 13

Girls: Little Bits of Heaven

*A man who has only sons
and who has never fathered
a daughter has lost a little
bit of Heaven on earth.*
  –Irish Proverb

No father has really tasted the thrill of fatherhood until his
six-year-old daughter starts waiting on him hand-and-foot.
  O.A. Battista

A girl is Innocence playing in the mud, Beauty standing on
its head, and Motherhood dragging a doll by the foot.
  Allan Beck

Little girls are the nicest things that happen to people.
  Allan Beck

A trick that everyone abhors
In little girls is slamming doors.
  Hilaire Belloc

This is the third of four daughters [to get engaged]. Every
time it happens, I'm obsessed with the feeling that I'm giving a million-dollar Stradivarius to a gorilla.
  Jim Bishop

Secrets with girls, like loaded guns with boys,
Are never valued till they make a noise.
  George Crabbe

It is only rarely that one can see in a little boy the promise

of a man, but one can almost always see in a little girl the threat of a woman.
Alexandre Dumas

To an old father, nothing is more sweet than a daughter.
Euripides

He's the type of guy I'd be proud to have as a son-in-law, just not with my daughter.
Peter Fritsch

Girls like to be played with, and rumpled a little, too, sometimes.
Oliver Goldsmith

What do little girls talk about?
  What is their mystic theme?
Those still too young for puppy love,
  Yet old enough to dream.
William Herschell

Boys will be boys, and even that...wouldn't matter if we could only prevent girls from being girls.
Anthony Hope

There was a little girl
Who had a little curl
Right in the middle of her forehead;
And when she was good,
She was very, very good,
But when she was bad she was horrid.
Henry Wadsworth Longfellow

One of life's unsolved mysteries is what young girls giggle about.
E.C. McKenzie

Kids Are *Tremendous!*

A girl is a girl so frilly and sweet
You'd just like to hug her the moment you meet.
She's little pink ruffles and nylon and lace;
She's an innocent look on a little pink face;
...She's kittens and everything cuddly and nice –
Ah, sure 'n she's a bit of God's own paradise.
Phyllis C. Michael

You cannot hammer a girl into anything. She grows as a flower does.
John Ruskin

Big sisters are the crabgrass in the lawn of life.
Charles Schulz (Charlie Brown - Peanuts)

If you destroy delicacy and a sense of shame in a young girl you deprave her very fast.
Harriet Beecher Stowe

Philosophers dispute whether it is the promise of what she will be...that makes her attractive, the undeveloped maidenhood, or the natural, careless sweetness of childhood.
Mark Twain

A daughter is mystery and enchantment and magic and fantasy all rolled up in a small, strange package.
Dan Valentine

The whisper of a pretty daughter can be heard above the roar of a mighty storm.
Hungarian Proverb

It is easier to watch over one hundred fleas than one young girl.
Polish Proverb

Kids Are *Tremendous!*

He who has daughters is always a shepherd.
Spanish Proverb

The lucky man has a daughter for his first-born.
Spanish Proverb

Raise your daughter to know the Lord and she will have a built-in chaperon.
Source Unknown

What are little girls made of?
Sugar and spice, and everything nice;
That's what little girls are made of.
Source Unknown

Chapter 14

Boys: No Experience Needed

One of the best things in the world is to be a boy; it requires no experience, but needs some practice to be a good one.
–Charles Dudley Warner

Boys naturally look on all force as an enemy.
Henry Adams

I don't want to go to school and learn solemn things. No one is going to catch me, lady, and make me a man. I want always to be a little boy and to have fun.
James M. Barrie (Peter Pan)

He was the spirit of boyhood, tugging at the skirts of this old world and compelling it to come back to play.
James M. Barrie (of Robert Louis Stevenson)

A boy is a magical creature—you can lock him out of your workshop, but you can't lock him out of your heart.
Allan Beck

A boy is a piece of existence quite separate from all things else and deserves separate chapters in the natural history of man.
Henry Ward Beecher

Whatever good there is in small boys is usually based upon their admiration for girls of their own age.
Arthur Brisbane

Kids Are *Tremendous!*

Golf...is a trifling thing beside the privilege of taking a small son to the zoo and letting him see his first lion, his first tiger and, best of all, his first elephant. Probably he will think that they are part of your own handiwork turned out for his pleasure...Cortez on his lonely peak in Darien was a pigmy discoverer beside the child eating his first spoonful of ice cream.
  Heywood Broun

I am fond of children—except boys.
  Lewis Carroll

I'm convinced that every boy, in his heart, would rather steal second base than an automobile.
  Justice Tom Clark

Boys do not grow up gradually. They move forward in spurts like the hands of clocks in railway stations.
  Cyril Connolly

Never be surprised when you shake a cherry tree if a boy drops out of it; never be disturbed when you think yourself in complete solitude if you discover a boy peering out at you from a fence corner.
  David Grayson

A fairly bright boy is far more intelligent and far better company than the average adult.
  J.B.S. Haldane

When I grow up I want to be a little boy.
  Joseph Heller

A boy becomes an adult three years before his parents think he does, and about two years after he thinks he does.
  General Lewis B. Hershey

Kids Are *Tremendous!*

A boy is a man in a cocoon—you do not know what it is going to become—his life is big with many possibilities.
　　Elbert Hubbard

Be patient with the boys—you are dealing with soul-stuff. Destiny awaits just around the corner.
　　Elbert Hubbard

Little boys may be an intolerable nuisance; but when they are not there we regret them, we find ourselves homesick for their very intolerableness.
　　Aldous Huxley

A Little Boy In Church
He ruffles through his hymn book,
He fumbles with his tie,
He laces up his oxfords,
He overworks a sigh;
He goes through all his pockets,
Engrossed in deep research;
There's no one quite so busy
As a little boy in church.
　　Thelma Ireland

Kaplan's Law of the Instrument: Give a small boy a hammer and he will find that everything he encounters needs pounding.
　　Abraham Kaplan

Boys are capital fellows in their own way, among their mates; but they are unwholesome companions for grown people.
　　Charles Lamb

Of all the animals, the boy is the most unmanageable.
　　Plato

Kids Are *Tremendous!*

Schoolboys have no fear of facing life. They chomp at the bit. The jealousies, the trials, the sorrows of the life of man do not intimidate the schoolboy.
Antoine de Saint-Exupéry

You save an old man and you save a unit; but save a boy, and you save a multiplication table.
Rodney "Gipsy" Smith

Do but gain a boy's trust; convince him by your behaviour that you have his happiness at heart; let him discover that you are the wiser of the two; let him experience the wisdom of following your advice and the evils that arise from disregarding it; and fear not you will readily enough guide him.
Herbert Spencer

The sweetest roamer is a boy's young heart.
G.E. Woodberry

A boy is a stick of dynamite, a bundle of energy and potential power, waiting to be ignited.
Optimist Magazine

Many a small boy is the kind of kid his mother wouldn't want him to play with.
Source Unknown

A boy is a noise with some dirt on it.
Source Unknown

Boys will be noise.
Source Unknown

When a small boy puts something down in black and white,

it's apt to be a towel.
Source Unknown

Home, to the small boy, is merely a filling station.
Source Unknown

Boy defined: Nature's answer to that false belief that there is no such thing as perpetual motion. A boy can swim like a fish, run like a deer, climb like a squirrel, balk like a mule, bellow like a bull, eat like a pig, or act like a jackass, according to climatic conditions. He is a piece of skin stretched over an appetite; a noise covered with smudges...He is a growing animal of superlative promise, to be fed, watered, and kept warm, a joy forever, a periodic nuisance, the problem of our times, the hope of a nation.
Source Unknown

Chapter 15

Grandkids: God's Compensation

Grandchildren are God's
way of compensating us for
growing old.
–Mary H. Waldrip

Grandbabies are better than babies. You can tote them around the church, collecting compliments, whereas it would be unseemly if you were merely the father.

Oren Arnold

Grandchildren don't make a man feel old; it's the knowledge that he's married to a grandmother.

G. Norman Collie

Nobody can do for little children what grandparents do. Grandparents sort of sprinkle stardust over the lives of little children.

Alex Haley

Nothing makes a child as smart as having grandparents.

Franklin P. Jones

There's nothing like having grandchildren to restore your faith in heredity.

Doug Larson

Few things are more delightful than grandchildren fighting over your lap.

Doug Larson

The reason grandparents and grandchildren get along so

well is that they have a common enemy.
Sam Levenson

The simplest toy, which even the youngest child can operate, is called a grandparent.
Sam Levenson

A grandmother is a person with too much wisdom to let that stop her from making a fool of herself over her grandchildren.
Phil Moss

Our children are here to stay, but our babies and toddlers and preschoolers are gone as fast as they can grow up—and we have only a short moment with each. When you see a grandfather take a baby in his arms, you see that the moment hasn't always been long enough.
St. Clair Adams Sullivan

Our lives revolved around education… Indeed, my grandfather announced that if we died, he would take us to school for three consecutive days to make sure that we were not faking.
Clarence Thomas

Perfect love does not come till the first grandchild.
Welsh Proverb

One thing you can say for small children—they don't go around showing off pictures of their grandparents.
Source Unknown

Chapter 16

Youth: Vanguard of Tomorrow

*Teenagers are the vanguard
of tomorrow. They are a
fresh breeze in a stale world.*
–Dan Valentine

Any astronomer can predict with absolute accuracy just where every star in the heavens will be at half-past eleven tonight. He can make no such prediction about his young daughter.
James Truslow Adams

There's one advantage to the music the younger generation goes for today – nobody can whistle it.
Roger Allen

As I vaguely recalled from my own experience, adolescence was a time…when the very idea that anything interesting might have happened during your parents' lifetime was unthinkable.
Russell Baker

Most of the criticism adults make about teenagers stems from envy.
O. A. Battista

You never know how wonderful the youth of America really are until you turn off the television and talk to them.
O. A. Battista

Most teenagers think that their family circle is composed of squares.
Dan Bennett

Kids Are *Tremendous!*

Mother Nature is providential. She gives us twelve years to develop a love for our children before turning them into teenagers.
Eugene P. Berlin

If you want to recapture your youth, cut off his allowance.
Al Bernstein

At 19, everything is possible and tomorrow is friendly.
Jim Bishop

By the time parents are ready to enjoy the comforts of life, their children are using them.
Bob Brown

One good thing about being young is that you are not experienced enough to know you cannot possibly do the things you are doing.
Gene Brown

The young do not know enough to be prudent, and therefore they attempt the impossible—and achieve it, generation after generation.
Pearl Buck

Adolescence is just one big walking pimple.
Carol Burnett

The best thing about being young is, if you had it to do all over again, you would still have time.
Sandra Clarke

Youth is when you blame all your troubles on your parents; maturity is when you learn that everything is the fault of the younger generation.
Harold Coffin

Kids Are *Tremendous!*

No man knows his true character until he has run out of gas, purchased something on the installment plan and raised an adolescent.
Marcelene Cox

That's what being young is all about. You have the courage and the daring to think that you can make a difference.
Ruby Dee

Telling a teenager the facts of life is like giving a fish a bath.
Arnold H. Glasow

Never tell a young person that anything cannot be done. God may have been waiting for centuries for somebody ignorant enough of the impossible to do that very thing.
John Andrew Holmes

Every young man should learn to take criticism. He'll probably be a parent someday.
Franklin P. Jones

Youth is looking for new answers—so they can question them.
Walt Kelly

Remember that as a teenager you are in the last stage of your life when you will be happy that the phone is for you.
Fran Lebowitz

One of the virtues of being very young is that you don't let the facts get in the way of your imagination.
Sam Levenson

There's nothing wrong with teenagers that reasoning won't aggravate.
H.E. Martz

Kids Are *Tremendous!*

A baby-sitter is a teenager who comes in to act like an adult while the adults go out and act like teenagers.
Henry Mason

Each youth is like a child born in the night who sees the sun rise and thinks that yesterday never existed.
W. Somerset Maugham

If you have teenagers in your house, you'll find it difficult to understand how farmers could possibly grow a surplus of food.
Vern McLellan

Youth do not think into the future far enough. There are great tomorrows we must encourage youth to dream of.
Henrietta C. Mears

Teenagers haven't changed much. They still grow up, leave home and get married. The big difference is that today they don't always do it in that order.
Herbert Miller

If you think there are no new frontiers, watch a boy ring the front doorbell on his first date.
Olin Miller

To get his teenage son to clean his room, one father just throws the keys to the family car in there once a week.
Lane Olinghouse

Teenagers are upset these days because they're living in a world dominated by nuclear weapons – and adults are upset because they're living in a world dominated by teenagers.
Robert Orben

Kids Are *Tremendous!*

It helps to think of rock music as youth's way of getting even for spinach.
Robert Orben

Oh, to be only half as wonderful as my child thought I was when he was small, and only half as stupid as my teenager now thinks I am.
Rebecca Richards

Adolescence is perhaps nature's way of preparing parents to welcome the empty nest.
Karen Savage and Patricia Adams

Don't laugh at a youth for his affectations; he is only trying on one face after another to find a face of his own.
Logan Pearsall Smith

If Abraham's son had been a teenager, it wouldn't have been a sacrifice.
Scott Spendlove

What are our young people coming to? Slowly, but surely, to the time when they will ask the same question.
H.M. Stansifer

I like teenagers. It would be a sorry, stagnant, boring, stand-still world without them.
Dan Valentine

In conversing with teenagers, parents envy the United Nations those earphones which give instant, simultaneous translations.
Bill Vaughn

The older generation thought nothing of getting up at five

every morning—and the younger generation doesn't think much of it either.
John J. Welsh

To grown people a girl of fifteen and a half is a child still; to herself she is very old and very real; more real, perhaps, than ever before or after.
Margaret Widdemer

Snow and adolescence are the only problems that disappear if you ignore them long enough.
Earl Wilson

Life goes on and there comes a time when you don't have to pay girls to spend the evening with your son.
Gene Yasenak

The person who says youth is a state of mind invariably has more state of mind than youth.
American Farm & Home Almanac

There is no vehicle that goes faster than youth.
Yiddish Folk Saying

There's nothing wrong with teenagers that reasoning with them won't aggravate.
Source Unknown

Since teenagers are too old to do the things kids do and not old enough to do the things adults do, they do things nobody else does.
Source Unknown

To many of today's parents, youth is stranger than fiction.
Source Unknown

Kids Are *Tremendous!*

The first man to tear a telephone book in half undoubtedly was the father of a teenager.

Source Unknown

Adolescents: Children who are old enough to dress themselves if they could just remember where they last saw their clothes.

Source Unknown

Heredity is what makes the parents of teenagers wonder a little about each other.

Source Unknown

Chapter 17

Some "Handy" Advice

*Never raise your hand to
your children—it leaves
your midsection unprotected.*
–Robert Orben

The best inheritance a parent can give to his children is a few minutes of his time each day.
O.A. Battista

You cannot teach a child to take care of himself unless you will let him try to take care of himself. He will make mistakes; and out of these mistakes will come his wisdom.
Henry Ward Beecher

The best way to train up a child the way he should go is to travel that road occasionally yourself.
Josh Billings

Never lend your car to anyone to whom you have given birth.
Erma Bombeck

Never have more children than you have car windows.
Erma Bombeck

Never reprimand a boy in the evening—darkness and a troubled mind are a poor combination.
Frank L. Boyden

Never fear spoiling children by making them too happy.

Kids Are *Tremendous!*

Happiness is the atmosphere in which all good affections grow.
Ann Eliza Bray

Never threaten your child with a visit to the dentist.
Jane E. Brody

People murder a child when they tell it to keep out of the dirt. In dirt is life.
George Washington Carver

The work will wait while you show the child the rainbow, but the rainbow won't wait while you do the work.
Patricia Clafford

One way you can often do more for your child is to do less.
Frank A. Clark

There are three ways to get something done: do it yourself, hire someone, or forbid your kids to do it.
Monta Crane

The difficult thing about children is that they come with no instructions. You pretty well have to assemble them on your own.
Dr. James Dobson

If you want to see what children can do, you must stop giving them things.
Norman Douglas

Let us teach our children to study man as well as mathematics and to build cathedrals as well as power stations.
David Eccles

Kids Are *Tremendous!*

Respect the child. Be not too much his parent. Trespass not on his solitude.
Ralph Waldo Emerson

Let your children go if you want to keep them.
Malcolm Forbes

Let thy child's first lesson be obedience, and the second will be what thou wilt.
Benjamin Franklin

The best time to tackle a minor problem is before he grows up.
Ray Freedman

If you want children to improve, let them overhear the nice things you say about them to others.
Haim Ginott

Never try to make your son or daughter another you; one is enough.
Arnold H. Glasow

If your whole world is upside down and joy and cheer are far from you, romp for an hour with a six-year-old child and see if its laughter and faith are not veritable sign posts on the Road to Happiness.
Gladys Harvey-Knight

If you would influence your child for good, let your presence radiate smiles. Let your children hear you laugh often; but laugh with them, never at them.
Gladys Harvey-Knight

Do not handicap your children by making their lives easier.
Robert A. Heinlein

Kids Are *Tremendous!*

Feel the dignity of a child. Do not feel superior to him, for you are not.
Robert Henri

The worst waste of breath, next to playing a saxophone, is advising a son.
Kin Hubbard

Don't forget that you are, or ought to be, your children's ideal of all that is perfection, and that it is your duty to live up to those ideals in every possible way. Not an easy task, but wonderfully inspiring.
Mrs. G.E. Jackson

At every step the child should be allowed to meet the real experiences of life; the thorns should never be plucked from the roses.
Ellen Key

Remember, when they have a tantrum, don't have one of your own.
Dr. Judith Kuriansky

Never allow your child to call you by your first name. He hasn't known you long enough.
Fran Lebowitz

Ask your child what he wants for dinner only if he's buying.
Fran Lebowitz

I do beseech you to direct your efforts more to preparing youth for the path and less to preparing the path for the youth.
Ben Lindsey

Kids Are *Tremendous!*

One of the most important things to remember about infant care is: never change diapers in midstream.
Don Marquis

Note on church bulletin board: "Parents, be the soul support of your children."
Vern McLellan

Never help a child with a task at which he feels he can succeed.
Maria Montessori

Perhaps parents would enjoy their children more if they stopped to realize that the film of childhood can never be run through for a second showing.
Evelyn Nown

When you are dealing with a child, keep all your wits about you, and sit on the floor.
Austin O'Malley

The best way to bring up some children is short.
Anthony J. Pettito

Fill a child's bucket of self-esteem so high that the rest of the world can't poke enough holes in it to drain it dry.
Alvin Price

All children wear the sign: "I want to be important NOW." Many of our juvenile delinquency problems arise because nobody reads the sign.
Dan Pursuit

If you want your child to walk the righteous path, do not merely point the way—lead the way.
J.A. Rosenkranz

Kids Are *Tremendous!*

Never show a child what he cannot see...While you are thinking about what will be useful to him when he is older, talk to him of what he can use now.
Jean-Jacques Rousseau

Have children while your parents are still young enough to take care of them.
Rita Rudner

You don't raise heroes, you raise sons. And if you treat them like sons, they'll turn out to be heroes, even if it's just in your own eyes.
Walter Schirra, Sr.

If you must hold yourself up to your children, hold yourself up as an object lesson and not as an example.
George Bernard Shaw

Train your child in the way you now know you should have gone yourself.
Charles H. Spurgeon

Kindly interest will do more to attract children than stately majesty.
Theodore G. Stelzer

I have found that the best way to give advice to your children is to find out what they want, and then advise them to do it.
Harry S. Truman

Never have children, only grandchildren.
Gore Vidal

If you want a baby, have a new one. Don't baby the old one.

Jessamyn West

If thine enemy wrong thee, buy each of his children a drum.

African Proverb

Do not confine your children to your own learning, for they were born in another time.

Chinese Proverb

If you don't want your children to hear what you're saying, pretend you're talking to them.

Source Unknown

Bear in mind that children of all ages have one thing in common—they close their ears to advice and open their eyes to example.

Source Unknown

Chapter 18

Kids on Wry

Ah, the patter of little feet
around the house. There's
nothing like having a midget
for a butler.
–W.C. Fields

When I was born I was so surprised I didn't talk for a year
and a half.
Gracie Allen

The person who invented summer camps ought to get the
Nobel Peace Prize.
Roger Allen

I am serious about wishing I had children, beautiful children. I wouldn't care for the other variety.
Tallulah Bankhead

If a woman has to choose between catching a fly ball and
saving an infant's life, she will choose to save the infant's
life without even considering if there are men on base.
Dave Barry

The fact that boys are allowed to exist at all is evidence of a
remarkable Christian forbearance among men.
Ambrose Bierce

I take a very practical view of raising children. I put a sign
in each of their rooms: "Checkout time is 18 years."
Erma Bombeck

Kids Are *Tremendous!*

When my kids become wild and unruly, I use a nice, safe playpen. When they're finished, I climb out.
Erma Bombeck

In general my children refused to eat anything that hadn't danced on TV.
Erma Bombeck

A child develops individuality long before he develops taste. I have seen my kid straggle into the kitchen in the morning with outfits that needed only one accessory: an empty gin bottle.
Erma Bombeck

The only time the average child is as good as gold is on April 15.
Ivern Boyett

Reasoning with a child is fine, if you can reach the child's reason without destroying your own.
John Mason Brown

Kids really brighten a household. They never turn off the lights.
Ralph Bus

My mom was fair. You never knew whether she was going to swing with her right or her left.
Herb Caen

I was so naïve as a kid I used to sneak behind the barn and do nothing.
Johnny Carson

As parents, my wife and I have one thing in common.

Kids Are *Tremendous!*

We're both afraid of children.
Bill Cosby

The first half of our lives is ruined by our parents and the second half by our children.
Clarence Darrow

Cleaning out the kids' room while they're still at home is like shoveling your sidewalk while it's still snowing.
Phyllis Diller

The babe, with a cry brief and dismal,
Fell into the water baptismal;
E're they'd gathered its plight,
It had sunk out of sight,
For the depth of the font was abysmal.
Edward Gorey

My parents were too poor to have children, so the neighbors had me.
Buddy Hackett

Perhaps one way of coping with the population explosion would be to give every potential parent some experience in driving a school bus.
Franklin P. Jones

Children are a great comfort in your old age and they help you to reach it, too.
Lionel Kaufman

The secret of dealing successfully with a child is not to be its parent.
Mell Lazarus

Kids Are *Tremendous!*

The parent who could see his boy as he really is would shake his head and say: "Willy is no good: I'll sell him."
Stephen Leacock

All God's children are not beautiful. Most of God's children are, in fact, barely presentable.
Fran Lebowitz

Insanity is hereditary; you can get it from your children.
Sam Levenson

If a child shows himself incorrigible, he should be decently and quietly beheaded at the age of twelve, lest he grow to maturity, marry, and perpetuate his kind.
Don Marquis

In order to influence a child, one must be careful not to be that child's parent or grandparent.
Don Marquis

When children are seen and not heard it's apt to be through binoculars.
E.C. McKenzie

I love children—especially when they cry, for then someone takes them away.
Nancy Mitford

Having children is like having a bowling alley installed in your brain.
Martin Mull

Parents were invented to make children happy by giving them something to ignore.
Ogden Nash

Kids Are *Tremendous!*

Oh, what a tangled web do parents weave
When they think their children are naïve.
Ogden Nash [attributed]

Do your kids a favor—don't have any.
Robert Orben

Even very young children need to be informed about death. Explain the concept of death very carefully to your child. This will make threatening him with it much more effective.
P.J. O'Rourke

The best way to keep children at home is to make the home atmosphere pleasant—and let the air out of the tires.
Dorothy Parker

Nature makes boys and girls lovely to look upon so they can be tolerated until they acquire some sense.
William Lyons Phelps

Of all the things I dislike, there is nothing so abhorrent to me as a spoilt child. I have pinched several, and never had the slightest qualm of conscience afterwards; and though I am a man of peace, I hope to pinch many more before I die.
H.L.R. Sheppard

Blessed is the man who does not insist upon talking about his children when I want to talk about mine.
Roy L. Smith

I first gave it a dose of castor oil, and then I christened it; so now the poor child is ready for either world.
Sydney Smith

Kids Are *Tremendous!*

How can a society that exists on instant mashed potatoes, packaged cake mixes, frozen dinners and instant cameras teach patience to its young?
Paul Sweeney

Familiarity breeds children.
Mark Twain

A soiled baby with a neglected nose cannot be conscientiously regarded as a thing of beauty.
Mark Twain

Teach a child to be polite and courteous in the home, and, when he grows up, he will never be able to edge his car onto a freeway.
Bill Vaughn

An ugly baby is a very nasty object, and the prettiest is frightful when undressed.
Queen Victoria

I don't like the size of them; the scale is all wrong. The heads tend to be too big for the bodies and the hands and feet are a disaster and they keep falling into things...they should be neither seen nor heard. And no one must make another one.
Gore Vidal

People who get nostalgic about childhood were obviously never children.
Bill Watterson

His mother should have thrown him away and kept the stork.
Mae West

Kids Are *Tremendous!*

It's a little frustrating sometimes when you listen to your children saying their prayers. It costs thousands and thousands of dollars to raise them and you get mentioned ahead of the goldfish but after the gerbil.

Pat Williams and Ken Hussar

There's a new baby food on the market. It's half orange juice and half garlic. It not only makes the baby healthier, but also easier to find in the dark.

Source Unknown

Children are natural mimics—they act like their parents in spite of every attempt to teach them good manners.

Source Unknown

School days can be the happiest days of your life, provided the children are old enough to go.

Source Unknown

If you want your child to follow in your footsteps, you've probably forgotten a few you took.

Source Unknown

Don't be discouraged if your children reject your advice. Years later they will offer it to their own offspring.

Source Unknown

The man who steps into a cage with a dozen lions impresses everybody except a school bus driver.

Source Unknown

Chapter 19

God's Apostles

Children: God's apostles,
day by day sent forth to
preach of love, and hope,
and peace.
–James Russell Lowell

The religion of Jesus is the religion of a little child. There is no affectation about a disciple of Jesus, he is as a little child, amazingly simple but unfathomably deep. Many of us are not childlike enough, we are childish.

Oswald Chambers

When once we are related to Jesus Christ, our relation to actual life is that of a child, perfectly simple and marvellous.

Oswald Chambers

I believe in little children as the most precious gift of Heaven to earth. I believe that they have immortal souls created in the image of God, coming forth from him and to return to him. I believe that in every child are infinite possibilities for good and evil and that the kind of influence with which he is surrounded in early childhood largely determines whether or not the budding life shall bloom in fragrance and beauty with the fruits thereof, a noble Godlike character.

Randall J. Condon

It is good to be children sometimes, and never better than at Christmas, when its mighty Founder was a child himself.

Charles Dickens

Kids Are *Tremendous!*

They are idols of hearts and of households;
They are angels of God in disguise;
His sunlight still sleeps in their tresses,
His glory still gleams in their eyes;
Those truants from home and from Heaven
They have made me more manly and mild;
And I know now how Jesus could liken
The kingdom of God to a child.
Charles M. Dickinson

When the lessons and tasks are all ended,
And the school for the day is dismissed,
The little ones gather around me,
To bid me good-night and be kissed;
On, the little white arms that encircle
My neck in their tender embrace
Oh, the smiles that are halos of heaven,
Shedding sunshine of love on my face.
Charles M. Dickinson

God sends children for another purpose than merely to keep
up the race—to enlarge our hearts; and to make us unselfish
and full of kindly sympathies and affections; to give our
souls higher aims; to call out all our faculties to extended
enterprise and exertion; and to bring round our firesides
bright faces, happy smiles, and tender, loving hearts. My
soul blesses the great Father, every day, that He has glad-
dened the earth with little children.
Mary Howitt

Children know the grace of God
Better than most of us.
They see the world
The way the morning brings it back to them,

Kids Are *Tremendous!*

New and born and fresh and wonderful.
Archibald MacLeish

There's a Friend for little children
Above the bright blue sky,
A Friend who never changes,
Whose love can never die.
Albert Midlane

The smallest children are nearest to God, as the smallest
planets are nearest the sun.
Jean Paul Richter

If there is anything that will endure
The eye of God, because it still is pure,
It is the spirit of a little child,
Fresh from his hand, and therefore undefiled.
Richard Henry Stoddard

Where children are not, heaven is not.
Algernon Swinburne

Every child comes with the message that God is not yet
discouraged of man.
Rabindranath Tagore

Hush, my dear, lie still and slumber,
Holy angels guard thy bed!
Heavenly blessings without number
Gently falling on thy head.
Isaac Watts

Gentle Jesus, meek and mild,
Look upon a little child,
Pity my simplicity,

Suffer me to come to Thee.
Charles Wesley

Every child born into the world is a new thought of God, an
ever-fresh and radiant possibility.
Kate Douglas Wiggin

An angel passed in his onward flight,
With a seed of love and truth and light,
And cried, O where shall the seed be sown –
That it yield most fruit when fully grown?
The Saviour heard and He said, as He smiled,
Place it for me in the heart of a child.
Source Unknown

Children's Beatitudes
Blessed is the child who has someone who believes in him,
to whom he can carry his problems unafraid.

Blessed is the child who is allowed to pursue his curiosity
into every worthwhile field of information.

Blessed is the child who has someone who understands that
childhood's griefs are real and call for understanding and
sympathy.

Blessed is the child who has about him those who realize
his need of Christ as Saviour and will lead him patiently
and prayerfully to the place of acceptance.

Blessed is the child whose love of the true, the beautiful
and the good has been nourished through the years.

Blessed is the child whose imagination has been turned into
channels of creative effort.

Kids Are *Tremendous!*

Blessed is the child whose efforts to achieve have found encouragement and kindly commendation.

Blessed is the child who has learned freedom from selfishness through responsibility and cooperation with others.
Source Unknown

Our children are the only possessions we can take to heaven.
Source Unknown

Some would gather money
Along the path of life.
Some would gather roses
And rest from worldly strife,
But I would gather children
From among the thorns of sin;
I would seek a golden curl
And a freckled, toothless grin.

For money cannot enter
In that land of endless day,
And the roses that are gathered
Soon will wilt along the way.
But, oh, the laughing children,
As I cross the Sunset Sea
And the gates swing wide to heaven,
I can take them in with me.
Source Unknown

Are All The Children In?
I think oftimes as the night draws nigh
Of an old house on the hill,
Of a yard all wide and blossom-starred
Where the children played at will.

Kids Are *Tremendous!*

And when the night at last came down,
Hushing the merry din,
Mother would look around and ask,
"Are all the children in?"

'Tis many and many a year since then,
And the old house on the hill
No longer echoes to childish feet,
And the yard is still, so still.
But I see it all as the shadows creep,
And though many the years have been,
Even now, I can hear my mother ask,
"Are all the children in?"

I wonder if, when the shadows fall
On the last short, earthly day,
When we say goodbye to the world outside,
All tired with our childish play,
When we step out into that Other Land
Where mother so long has been,
When we hear her ask, as we did of old,
"Are all the children in?"

And I wonder, too, what the Lord will say,
To us older children of His,
Have we cared for the lambs? Have we showed them the fold?
A privilege joyful it is.
And I wonder, too, what our answers will be,
When His loving questions begin:
"Have you heeded my voice? Have you told of my love?
Have you brought My children in?"

Source Unknown (last verse by Marion Bishop
Bower)

Chapter 20

Letter to a Grandson

When my first grandson was still a young boy, I wrote this letter to share with him some of the wonderful life lessons I've been learning.
–Charlie "Tremendous" Jones

My Dear Sammy,

Each word in this letter is bathed with my love and prayers for you. As you get older, you'll discover that your mind doesn't always keep pace with your body. This is because the food you eat feeds your body, but it's what you feed your mind and heart that determines your growth as a person.

I'm going to share a few principles that I pray you'll commit to memory. I could share many more, but I've tried to select those that I wish I could have begun working on earlier in my life.

READ, READ, READ, READ, READ

A proper diet is good for your body and the best books are good for your mind. Your life will be determined by the people you associate with and the books you read. Many people you'll come to love will be met in books. Read biographies, autobiographies and history. Your books will provide all the friends, mentors, role models and heroes you'll ever need.

Biographies will help you see there is nothing that can

happen to you that wasn't experienced by many who used their failures, disappointments and tragedies as stepping-stones to a more tremendous life. Many of my best friends are people I've never met: Oswald Chambers, George Mueller, Charles Spurgeon, A.W. Tozer, Abraham Lincoln, Robert E. Lee, François Fenelon, Jean Guyon and hundreds of others

Don't just READ the Bible. Study it! Digest it! Memorize it and realize God's greatest gift to our time on earth is His Word made flesh, and living in our hearts through Jesus Christ our Lord.

FORGIVE

Our unwillingness to forgive when we've been deeply hurt breeds self-pity and bitterness. If you'll learn and experience God's love and forgiveness through Jesus, you'll have no problem in forgiving anyone for anything. The hurt or injustices you experience will leave scars, but your life will be enriched by the joy of practicing what you've received.

PRAY

Praying is more than talking to God. Prayer is God's spirit speaking to you and for you and moving you to share your thoughts, problems and praise with Him. Never allow your unfaithfulness to keep you from praying. God always hears us as we pray in Jesus' name, because He is faithful. The right words never matter to God. He hears the words of your heart that can't be expressed in words and, best of all, the Holy Spirit is our interpreter.

Kids Are *Tremendous!*

GIVE

Never give to get, give because you've received. Giving is like a muscle. To be strong, you have to exercise it, and to grow as a person, giving is the exercise. You can't really enjoy anything without sharing it. This includes your faith, love, talents and money. Someday you'll discover we never really give, we're only returning and sharing a small portion of what we've received.

DECISIONS

The more decisions you make, the more tremendous your life will be. Don't wait for the right time; do something now, today! Don't worry about big decisions, make many little ones and the big ones will seem little. Your job is not to make a right decision as much as to make one and invest your life making it right.

You have only two big decisions in life—your marriage and your work. Don't look for what you'd like to do. Find something that needs to be done and prepare to do it. You'll discover the joy of doing something that ought to be done, while other are wasting their lives searching for something they'd like to do. Don't waste time looking for a better job. Do a better job and you'll have a better job.

Your marriage—Someday you'll meet someone to love and to share your life with. Love between and man and a woman is second only to the love of God, but there is one big difference. God's love never changes, while our love is very changeable. So please remember commitment in your marriage is more important than love.

Commitment will save your marriage when your love

dies or until it lives again. I thought God gave me your grandmother to love me but, over the years, God has shown me He gave her to me to learn to love even if she ceased loving me. You can do this only when you experience the love of Christ. Then and only then will it make sense.

THANKFUL

Learning to be thankful covers it all. "In everything give thanks for this is the will of God concerning you in Christ. You may not always be sure of God's will, and you may not always be sure you're doing God's will, but you can easily always *be His will* by thanking Him for all things.

You're thankful spirit should go beyond things, blessings, gifts and healing. Every breath you breathe will be filled with thankfulness when you realize Jesus Christ is your Blesser, Giver and Healer. I would encourage you to commit to memory A.B. Simpson's *Himself.*

When you have children of your own, I hope you'll give thanks for your food with them as we did with your dad: "Lord, we thank You for our food. But if we had none, we would thank you anyway. Because, Lord, we're not just thankful for what You give us. We're thankful most of all for the privilege of learning to be thankful."

There are thousands of other thoughts I would love to share with you, but I know God will be revealing them to your heart more wonderfully than any human tongue can tell. Remember:

> Learn to laugh at yourself;
> Learn to help others laugh;
> Learn to laugh when you're up;

Kids Are *Tremendous!*

Learn to laugh when you're down;
Learn to laugh.

Circumstances won't allow you to always be happy, but Jesus will help you look like you are.

I love you tremendously,

Your devoted grandfather

Chapter 21

Getting Kids to Read

"You are the same today as you'll be in five years, except for two things: the people you meet and the books you read."

By Charlie "Tremendous" Jones

I'll never forget the thrill I got when I read a book filled with tremendous truths that were completely opposite to what I had believed. After the first book, I found a string of them, and many of these terrific insights were first written fifty to one hundred years ago.

I began to share these ideas by buying the books in quantity and giving one to everyone who came to my office. If they didn't want to read—they got one anyway. I knew they'd get an impulse sometime to read, and these books would do more for them than a truckload of pills.

The books began to change my life and the lives of my friends and associates. Then I realized I'd overlooked the most important people in my life, my family. My oldest son Jere was fourteen at the time. I knew he'd rebel against my forcing him to read, so I planned some strategy. You know, you can lead a horse to water, but you can't make him drink—well, I decided to put some salt in Jere's oats and make him thirsty.

"Jere, in two years you're going to want me to help you

buy a car, and I want to help you. But I'm not going to give you the money. Here's my proposal: I'm going to pay you $10 for every book you read. I'll pick the book, you give me a written report, and I'll put $10 in a car fund."

It was all Jere needed to hear. Before long, he'd read 22 books. When he went off to college, he sent me a postcard every day telling me about the books he was reading and about the new ideas they gave him.

Over the years, I've shared some of these experiences with groups I've spoken to all over the world. So many asked me about my deal with Jere that I prepared the agreement form that follows (Appendix). I encourage you to use it with your own family members.

I once heard someone say: "You are the same today as you'll be in five years, except for two things: the people you meet and the books you read." Space doesn't allow me to list even a few of my favorite books here, but I encourage you to visit our website at www.executivebooks.com, where you'll find a wealth of information.

Happy reading!

Here are a few of Jere's postcards that show what books did for him—and his dad!

Dear Dad,

The only happy man, successful man, confident man or practical man is the one who is simple. SIB-KIS.* Unless his mind can crystallize all the answers into one powerful punch of personal motivation, he will live nothing but a life of uncertainty and fear.

(*See It Big—Keep It Simple)

Tremendously, too (Tt),
Jere

Dad,

It is tremendous to be able to know that when you are in a slump, just as the baseball player will break out in time, so you will break out of yours. Yes, time really cures things. Like you said, you don't lose any problems, you just get bigger and better ones. Tremendous ones!

Tt,
Jere

Dad,

Just started reading 100 Great Lives. Thanks for what you said in the front—the part that every great man never sought to be great; he just followed the vision he had and did what had to be done!

Love,
Jere

Dad,

Nothing new, just the same old exciting thought that we can know God personally and forever in this amazing life!

Jere

Kids Are *Tremendous!*

Dad,

I just got done typing up little quotes out of the Bible and Napoleon (Hill) so that everywhere I look I see them. When people ask what they are, I will tell them. They are my pin-ups.

Jere

Dad,

I am more convinced than ever that you can do anything you want; you can beat anyone at anything, just by working hard. Handicaps don't mean anything because often people who don't have them have a bad attitude and don't want to work.

Jere

Dad,

The mind of God is so unbelievable. He throws nothing but paradoxes at us. He makes us completely and utterly helpless and depraved; and then takes that failure which normally knocks us out—and makes it our greatest asset.

Jere

Dad,

When you're behind two papers in the fourth quarter, and you are exhausted from the game, and you have to make this set of downs in order to stay in the game, and you get up to the line and see five 250-lb. tests staring you in the mug, it sure is exciting to wait to find out what play the Lord will call next! WOW!

Jere

Book Report:
Acres of Diamonds
By Samuel Jones - Age 13

Acres of Diamonds is a lecture written by Russell H. Conwell first given in 1869 just a few years after the Civil War. It was delivered 6,152 times, the first time when he was only 16. There are many lessons to be learned and I'll share what I've gotten from this speech.

One thing I got from this is that you shouldn't leave one job until you have another one. Don't just get rid of a job because you don't like it or there are bigger and better things out there. Wait until you get another job first, or you might find yourself in a really bad position.

Another thing to do is to try to make money. Be pretty eager to get rich. You should because it is your Godly duty to try. The love of money is the root of all evil, not just money. You can do a lot more good with money than without it.

Do not think that making profit is wrong. You do not have the right to take losses. People will not trust you with money if you cannot manage yours, just like they wouldn't trust a known scammer or cheater.

This does not mean, however, that you can grab all the money you can get your hands on. Getting money by cheating others is not just sinning, it is idolatry. Going to the measure of lying to people to get money is putting money above God.

As I close, I would like to say some things about Acres of Diamonds. It mostly says that making money is not an evil thing to do, and then helps draw the lines as to what you can do and not go too far as to worship money. Conwell also reminds us that there are better things than money, and I believe that no one should forget about that.

Samuel Jones

Kids Are *Tremendous!*

CHARLES "TREMENDOUS" JONES
LETTER TO GRANDSON SAMMY

My dear Sammy,

No words can express how much I appreciated your tremendous book review of "Acres of Diamonds." You not only grasped the basic points but you discovered the spirit of money. Very few men much older than you have even discovered what you have.

I would remind you that reading this classic was a good experience but the time you spent thinking about it in order to write your thoughts made it an invaluable experience that will influence your actions the rest of your life.

Your next obligation will be to share some of your thoughts with some of your friends and even your teachers. One of the greatest joys of a teacher is a student sharing and discovering the laws of life and success. Also, you'll discover the joy of thinking new thoughts are more enjoyable and profitable when they are shared. Every time you share a great thought it becomes more real and you discover there is a lot more to learn about your discovery.

I'm enclosing one hundred dollars, a reward for your efforts. I would ask you to give the first $10.00 to your church, $10.00 for allowance and $80.00 for your college fund.

I'm enclosing a new little booklet called "Books are Tremendous." It includes many great authors and quotes of great leaders on their love for books. I had 16 college students spend the day with me yesterday. I had them read to me J.C. Penney's thoughts on the importance of reading for young people. Those young people will forget most of what I said but the thoughts we read together are now a part of their life forever.

Thank you for making me and your mother so happy and proud. Years from now you will discover the future happiness you've stored up for yourself when you remember how happy you made us.

I'm looking forward to your next book review. I know you are busy but remember the busiest people know we waste half of our time so I only ask you to use some of the time you normally waste, on reading, thinking, writing and sharing.

I love you tremendously,

CHARLES "TREMENDOUS" JONES
Your devoted grandfather,
Romans 10:17, Acts 20:24

Appendix—Kids Are *Tremendous!*

Agreement

*BECAUSE*_____*(adult)*
*and*_____ *(child) have agreed to certain things
regarding the reading of books and the reward for this reading, and*

BECAUSE this reading will increase _____*(child's)
store of knowledge, increase his/her ability to LEARN and to help
master the problems of living,* _____*(adult)
wishes to encourage this reading.*

THEREFORE, _____*(adult) agrees to
REWARD* _____*(child) for each book read that
is not part of regular school requirements. These are to be
_____(child's) choice of historical fiction,
autobiographies or similar books. The reward shall be $_____ for
each book read.*

*BECAUSE, in addition to teaching the value of books, this agreement
is designed to teach the values of thrift and helping others,
_____(child) agrees to:*

*Use the first ten percent (ten cents of each dollar) to help others.
Suggested uses are: Sunday School or church, United Way, Red
Cross, missionary work.*

*Deposit half of the remaining 90 percent (45 cents of each dollar) in
a bank account for future education or similar use.*

*Spend the remaining 45 cents as he or she sees fit, subject only to
parental guidance.*

*This agreement shall be in full force and effect when signed by both
parties and shall be effective for one year from the date shown below.
It shall be renewed each year unless either party notifies the other
that he or she wishes to cancel it.*

*Signed and agreed to this____ day of _____, in the Year of
Our Lord 20____ .*

_____

(print or sign – Child)

_____

(Signature – Adult)